The Prehistoric Temples of
STONEHENGE & AVEBURY

Keith Sugden

The Prehistoric Temples of
STONEHENGE & AVEBURY

Keith Sugden

A vebury and Stonehenge, the two most important prehistoric temples in Britain, are sited quite close together, about 28km apart. Why should this be? Although it may not be immediately apparent, they occupy a central position as far as ancient tracks are concerned. Many ridgeways converge on Salisbury Plain, following dry ridges free of natural dense woodland from Cornwall, the south coast, Kent, East Anglia, the Midlands, the North of England, and Wales. Their importance to prehistoric man is confirmed by evidence for long-distance trade along these routes. The most vital ridgeway of all was the Harroway (Hoar, or Hard, Way) along the Cretaceous chalk ridge of the North Downs from Dover to Stonehenge, because this was the main route for all Britain's immigrants from the continent of Europe – the Dover Straits was still a land-bridge until about 8000 BC. The focus of ridgeways is perhaps why Neolithic man chose the chalk downs of Wiltshire for the temple at Stonehenge, for the massive henge at Avebury, and for Silbury Hill, the largest prehistoric mound in Europe, looming 40m above the Bath road near Avebury. Bronze Age people built large numbers of barrows around these early sacred sites, as if in homage to the shrines of their predecessors.

LEFT:

RECONSTRUCTION (SALISBURY MUSEUM) OF A BEAKER BURIAL NEAR STONEHENGE, WITH POT AND BRONZE KNIFE.

RIGHT:

THIS AERIAL VIEW FROM THE NORTH SHOWS THE CENTRAL STONES SURROUNDED BY THE EARLIER BANK AND DITCH. THE SLAUGHTER STONE, THE LEANING HEEL STONE AND THE BANKS AT THE START OF THE AVENUE CAN BE SEEN NEAR THE ROAD.

STONEHENGE

Henges are lonely and inspiring pagan temples which never occur outside the British Isles. Nearly 100 henges survive, scattered as far apart as Cornwall and the Orkney Isles. But, above all, it is here in Wessex that henges are found: the four largest (Avebury, map reference SU103699, Durrington Walls, SU150437, Marden, SU091582, and Mount Pleasant, SY710899) as well as the two most famous, at Stonehenge and Avebury.

A henge is a circular or oval area defined by a bank and a ditch and approached by one or two entrances. The bank is usually outside the ditch, so that the bank forms the boundary to a sacred area, separated physically and spiritually from the everyday world. Stonehenge itself is a curiosity on two counts: its bank is inside the ditch and within the henge stands the most elaborate set of prehistoric stones in Europe. Stonehenge is eccentric, but nevertheless it has given its name to the whole group of monuments.

The sequence of construction at Stonehenge

Visitors always want to know when Stonehenge was built, but only recently have we been able to give the right answer. John Aubrey, in the 17th century, ascribed it to the 'ancient Britons' who lived here before the Roman invasion of AD 43; others attributed it to the Danes who followed the Romans; William Stukeley, in the 18th century, got carried away by his false Druidic fantasies and so started a misconception still current today. The first to establish the correct period was Professor William Gowland who, in 1901,

LEFT:

THE HEEL STONE, ORIGINALLY UPRIGHT, IS THE ONLY MEGA-LITH TO SURVIVE OUTSIDE THE DITCH OF THE HENGE. IT IS A LARGE UNWORKED SARSEN AND THE NEAREST SOURCE WOULD HAVE BEEN THE MARLBOROUGH DOWNS EAST OF AVEBURY, A JOURNEY OF SOME 36KM. ORIGINALLY A PAIR OF HEEL STONES FLANKED THE LINE TO THE MIDSUMMER SUNRISE.

NUMEROUS FINDS OF HUMAN BONE DEPOSITED IN EASTERN
SECTIONS OF STONEHENGE'S DITCH TESTIFY TO THE FUNER-
ARY ELEMENT IN THE PRACTICES THERE. THIS IMAGINARY
SCENE DEPICTS THE CENTRE OF THE HENGE AT DAYBREAK
ON THE SUMMER SOLSTICE. THE SUN RISES BETWEEN TWO
FORESIGHTS OUTSIDE THE SARSEN CIRCLE ON THE AXIS
MARKED C ON THE PHASE III PLAN. THIS ARTIST'S RECON-
STRUCTION IS BASED ON EVIDENCE FOR RITES OF HUMAN
SACRIFICE IN PREHISTORIC WESSEX WHICH IS DISCUSSED
FURTHER ON PAGE 12.

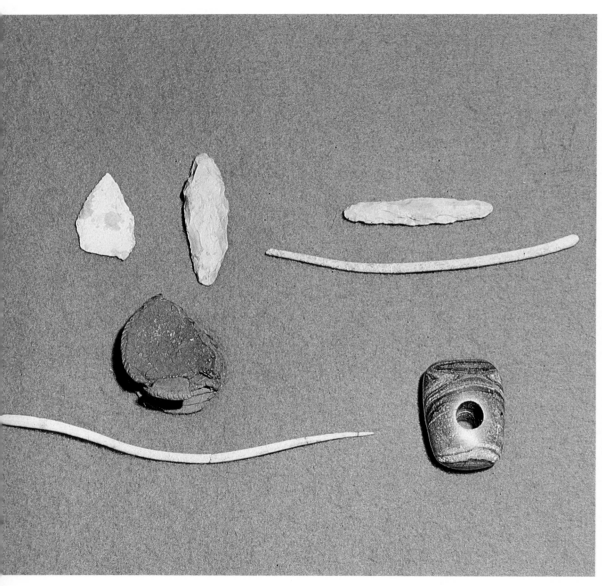

excavated the base of a leaning stone (No. 56) so carefully that he was able to conclude that Stonehenge had been constructed 'during the period of transition from stone to bronze'.

When Stonehenge passed into public ownership in 1918, the Society of Antiquaries supported a long campaign of excavations by Colonel William Hawley from 1919 to 1926. In many ways this was a disaster, because Hawley's patient but unthinking digging, only described in the briefest of published summaries, has wrecked the evidence for ever. The involvement of Professor Richard Atkinson from the late 1940s began with an attempt to recover the information lost by Hawley's endeavours and ended in triumph in 1963, with the whole sequence of construction clearly understood. Far from being built at one time, drastic remodelling of the monument had continued over some 1,700 years, straddling very broadly the 'transition from stone to bronze'.

Atkinson divided the sequence into four main phases which are clearly explained by the plans inside the front cover. In Phase I, corresponding to about 2800 BC, a rather modest henge about 91m across was dug, with a standard north-east entrance. For a Wessex henge, however, it already had unusual features: the bank inside the ditch, instead of the other way around, and a circle of 56 'Aubrey holes' dug just inside the bank. This date falls in the middle of the British Neolithic period and the characteristic finds here are fragments of pottery known to specialists as 'Grooved Ware' from their style of decoration. During Phase I the Heel Stone, which weighs about 35 tonnes, and its companion were erected like a gunsight just beyond the entrance to the henge.

Phase I may have ended with a time of abandonment: snails called 'Zonitidae' became abundant, indi-

ABOVE:

SARSEN HAMMERS USED TO SHAPE THE STONES. THE SMALL-
EST IS THE SIZE OF AN ORANGE.

RIGHT:

TWO OF THE TRILITHONS, SHOWING THE DOWNWARD TAPER
AND CURVATURE OF THE LINTELS. IN FRONT OF THEM STAND
TWO PILLARS OF THE BLUESTONE HORSE-SHOE. THE LARGE
FALLEN STONE, PAIRED WITH THE UPRIGHT ON THE LEFT,
FORMED THE CENTRAL TRILITHON. UNIQUELY, BOTH WERE
DRESSED SMOOTH ON THE OTHER SIDE.

cating that ungrazed grassland took over the site. In
the surrounding plain, tracts of formerly agricultural
land became a wilderness. Perhaps the henge continued to be used in a state of partial dereliction merely
as an enclosed cemetery. Hawley found about 30 cre-
mation burials from the later Neolithic cut into the
tops of the Aubrey holes. Then, in Phase II, c.2100 BC,
there were developments by the 'Beaker' people, so-
called from the characteristic shape of their pottery.
Their arrival marks the earliest phase of the Wessex
Bronze Age. A new north-easterly alignment was
emphasized by the Avenue, a broad embankment
extending 510m outside the ditch and still visible
today. The entrance to the henge had to be widened
by throwing down part of the bank to make it

7

symmetrical with this slightly different axis. The four Station Stones were placed in a huge rectangle which has an undoubted astronomical significance (see plan and p.14). At the same time the first of the mysterious bluestones were introduced as two modest circles in the centre of the henge, each with an entrance looking straight along the Avenue. These stones were later re-arranged within the Sarsen Circle.

It was, however, Phase III that made Stonehenge such a remarkable monument. Professor Atkinson discerned three separate episodes of remodelling. The first, known as IIIA and dated c.2000 BC, was the most spectacular and is the part that everybody remembers – the giant Trilithon Horseshoe and the Sarsen Circle around it. The geometry of the continuous lintel is truly amazing: it is accurately circular and precisely level despite the sloping site. Each component is cut to form a circular arc, linked to its neighbour by a vertical tongue-and-groove joint and held on its upright by a mortice-and-tenon joint. This daring and unique monument corresponds to far-reaching changes in society. The Bronze Age was not simply a time of advancing technology. Society underwent profound changes, particularly with the strong development of a hierarchy. Status became supremely important and this is reflected in the magnificent style of the burials.

Stonehenge is surrounded by scores of prominent round barrows where the chieftains and their queens were interred, for the first time in Britain, with valuable weapons and elaborate ornaments.

Phase IIIB followed in c.1550 BC, when the Y and Z holes were dug in concentric circles outside the settings of sarsens, and the bluestones were re-erected in an oval arrangement within the horseshoe. For some

LEFT:
THE SURVIVING UPRIGHT OF THE CENTRAL TRILITHON, THE TALLEST STONE AT STONEHENGE, WITH THE TENON ON TOP. THE FALLEN LINTEL, WITH MORTICES, LIES IN FRONT OF IT.
RIGHT:
THREE UPRIGHTS OF THE SARSEN CIRCLE, SHOWING THE UPWARD TAPER OF THEIR SHAPES.

reason the bluestones were moved again quite soon –
Phase IIIc is also dated c.1550 BC – this time to the
present setting of an oval between the Trilithon Horseshoe and the Sarsen Circle, plus a second horseshoe
nestling within the large one.

In Phase IV, dated c.1100 BC, the Avenue, already
1,000 years old, was extended by two straight
stretches for a further 2km. This brought it down to
meet the River Avon. The project, however, was abandoned before the inner ditch was dug. The outer ditch
was back-filled so that, unlike the earlier part of the
Avenue, the newer section can no longer be seen,
except from the air as a crop mark. It has been sug-
gested that the intended Avenue would have enshrined
the route taken by the magical bluestones after they
were unloaded from the River Avon. Associated with
this phase is a style of pottery ascribed by archaeologists to the 'Deverel-Rimbury' people, intensive farmers who introduced the ox-drawn plough. Their arrival
coincided with a great change in customs and beliefs.
The old gods, perhaps, had proved false. They and
their temple were abandoned, this time for ever.

Most visitors take for granted that the monument
should be so ruined: only a quarter of the Sarsen Circle
remains intact and what remains of the Trilithon
Horseshoe has been largely re-erected. Yet this assump-
tion may be wrong. After all, the method of construction of the Sarsen Circle was very sound, with all the
stones locked together by 'woodwork' joints and the
uprights socketed firmly in packed chalk. Solitary
megaliths all over Britain stay upright, so there is no
reason why Stonehenge should fall down, even after
4,000 years. A viable hypothesis is that some unknown
Roman general deliberately slighted the monument,
mistakenly believing that it was a stronghold of the
Druids, their fiercely independent opponents, who the
Romans condemned for practising human sacrifice.

The mystery of the bluestones

The origin of the bluestones, sometimes called 'foreign stones', of Stonehenge is highly evocative. Twenty-nine of the blocks are dolerite, a beautiful intrusive rock with highly unusual white or pink spots of albite-oligoclase felspar. Four more are rhyolite, a compact and light blue-grey volcanic rock, often conspicuously banded.

As long ago as 1858 Sir Andrew Ramsey noted their similarity to the Lower Silurian igneous rocks of north Pembrokeshire. Then, in 1923, Herbert Thomas, a petrographer with the Geological Survey, astounded the Society of Antiquaries with his proof of the actual source of the bluestones. He found outcrops of both the dolerite and the rhyolite, 'identical in the minutest detail' with his Stonehenge samples, on Mynydd Preseli (the Prescelly Mountains) of north Pembrokeshire. The occurrence of the outcrops of these highly individual rocks so close together is extremely suggestive of some special religious value or healing property having been attached to these particular stones and no others. The eastern Mynydd Preseli are themselves very rich in megalithic monuments – the remains of seven stone circles may still be found there today. Conceivably, the bluestones were originally erected on Mynydd Preseli and transported as an already venerated stone circle to Stonehenge.

We are left to explain how men moved the bluestones some 4,500 years ago. Thomas himself favoured a totally overland journey of about 290km but, by not specifying its course, he did not have the difficult task of defending his route in detail! Widely preferred today is the following water route of about 360km: (1) overland for about 15km from the outcrops to the navigable point of the Eastern Cleddau; (2) about 40km down the Eastern Cleddau; (3) about 185km up the Bristol Channel from Milford Haven to

RIGHT:
CURVED LINTELS OF THE OUTER CIRCLE, SHOWING A TONGUED JOINT TO LOCATE A MISSING LINTEL.

LEFT:
CARVINGS OF A BRONZE DAGGER AND AXE-HEADS ON THE INNER SIDE OF A TRILITHON.

Avonmouth; (4) about 50km up the Somerset Avon; (5) about 20km overland from Trowbridge to Heytesbury; (6) about 25km down the River Wylye; (7) about 20km up the Wiltshire Avon; and (8) about 3km along the Stonehenge Avenue.

The Stonehenge rituals

As a result of the Roman propaganda against the Celtic Druids, human sacrifice in prehistoric Britain has often been taken for granted. Now the excavators have provided proof. Among many cases are examples from both the Stonehenge and Avebury areas. In the open space at the centre of Woodhenge, an interesting site with open access 3km north-east of Stonehenge, was found the shallow grave of a 3½-year-old girl, facing the entrance and the rising sun. Her skull was neatly split in two by an axe. Another foundation sacrifice turned up at Avebury's Sanctuary: the body of an adolescent youth, aged 14 years, emphasized an important barrow alignment when the temple last rebuilt. Perhaps we condemn these practices too easily. 'Human sacrifice should not be equated with our modern attitude to murder', says Aubrey Burl in *Rites of the Gods*. 'It symbolized some need in society, whose urgency and necessity was more keenly stated if the chosen symbol was a human being.'

Another famous death is the 'Stonehenge murder': in 1978 the body of a tall strong man, aged about 27 years and dating from the earlier Bronze Age, was found in the ditch of the henge. There were three arrow-heads with the corpse, one buried in his sternum and another in a rib. The victim had been shot from close range and then treated with contempt, being thrown into a hastily-dug pit with the arrow-shafts still protruding from his body. When found he was still wearing his slate wrist-guard and so was presumably an archer himself.

The Stonehenge environs have now yielded many

ceremonial symbols to intrigue us. The chieftain buried under the Bush Barrow, for example, took with him to the Otherworld the symbols of his earthly power – a macehead of rare limestone, its shaft enriched by bone mounts, a bronze axe, and three copper and bronze daggers, one with a handle inlaid with thousands of minute gold pins – not to mention his earthly wealth expressed by hammered-gold belt ornaments. Maceheads and ceremonial axes of semi-precious stone, such as jadeite, played a central role in the priests' authority and rites. Carved on one of the trilithons (No. 53) are a clear dagger and axe-head, with less obvious groups of axes on stones No. 3 and No. 4. Buried in the Aubrey holes of the early henge were chalk balls and flint rods, understood by Burl to be phallic symbols. Less obvious are cups, which may be symbols of female sexuality.

The astronomer–priest theory

The late Professor Alexander Thom, although an engineer, spent much of his life trying to demonstrate that megalithic man built stone circles and rows to study solar and lunar astronomy. So well did he know their movements, claimed Thom, that he could predict which full or new moon would give rise to an eclipse of the moon or of the sun. Observations were made when objects rose or set and these points on the horizon were marked, according to the astronomical theory, either by stone alignments or by distant foresights, such as mounds or notches on the skyline. Thom surveyed Stonehenge and found no distant markers, concluding that here was an astronomical temple more for ceremony than for accurate observation.

Although many prominent archaeologists in the 1960s and 1970s challenged it, this theory has, broadly speaking, stood the test of time. The latest

research has shown that Stonehenge began as a lunar temple, but was later modified for worship of the sun. The four Station Stones, arranged during Phase II in a huge rectangle, indicate, with their long sides, the moon setting in its extreme north position. At the same time the rectangle's short sides indicate the midsummer sunrise. Only at, or close to, the latitude of Stonehenge will a rectangle fulfil this dual function. The original entrance from Phase I of the henge aligned with the most northerly rising of the moon, the 'major standstill'. Fifty three stake holes in six arcs have been found across the entrance to the henge. They were used during the century of observation which was required to define the bearing of 41°. This pre-occupation with the moon is probably connected with rituals of death. But quite soon the astronomer–priests changed their entrance to a bearing 9° further south, thus aligning the henge with the midsummer sunrise. As the priest performed his solstice rites at dawn in the exact centre of the temple he would see the sun rise exactly between the Heel Stone and its companion (No. 97).

Stonehenge: the ritual landscape

Stonehenge, of course, did not arise in splendid isolation. The modern visitor who stands and looks out onto Salisbury Plain can still see and explore monuments of the rich ritual landscape. Most obvious of all are the burial mounds of the Bronze Age élite. The nearest such round barrow is a mere 60m outside the henge. But cemeteries can be seen, sited on prominent ridges, in all directions: on the eastern horizon cluster the King barrows, to the northwest the Cursus barrows and, across the dry valley to the south, the Normanton Down barrows. Many more lie hidden, but all the Bronze Age types are there for the visitor to find in a morning's walk.

LEFT:

THE CENTRAL PILLAR OF THE BLUESTONE HORSESHOE OF PERIOD IIIc, NOW FALLEN, WITH TRACES OF A BATTERED-DOWN TENON ON THE NEAR END.

Over a dozen long barrows in the area precede Stonehenge, dating from c. 3700 to 3000 BC. Archaeologists, who used to see them as just tombs, now recognize, in the form of long barrows, territorial markers and the first temples. The best example is the founder member of the Winterbourne Stoke cemetery on the north-east side of the present A360/A303 roundabout, called Longbarrow Crossroads. Neolithic ideas on the disposal of the dead seem distinctly grisly today. People then believed that the spirit lingered in the corpse until all the flesh had been stripped from the bones. Only then could the bones be safely buried. Corpses had to be exposed for about two years to decay naturally. To prevent the bodies being ripped apart by scavengers, special mortuary houses were built. This is a favoured explanation for the elaborate post-holes found at nearby Woodhenge. Possibly Phase I of Stonehenge itself included a central wooden mortuary house.

The Cursus, a fine Neolithic monument, also pre-dates Stonehenge. As its true purpose still remains obscure, experts see it simply as 'ceremonial'. Death and its rituals, perhaps funeral processions or games, were somehow involved, judging from the way a long barrow formed its eastern terminus and round barrows cluster close by. The Cursus lies just 800m north of Stonehenge and extends for 2.7km, from the present Fargo Plantation, across a shallow dry valley, into the Larkhill Barracks. A visit to the Cursus itself, and the Cursus Barrows, forms a most rewarding short walk.

THE STONEHENGE PEOPLE

Who were the Stonehenge and Avebury people and how did they live? The early Wessex farmers chose the dry chalk uplands because it was easy to clear the forests with their polished stone axes and work the light soil with their simple wooden ploughs or 'ards'. We know what they ate from the remains of numerous feasts, such as those found in the Coneybury pit about 1km from Stonehenge – bones of cattle and roe deer, with some red deer, pig, beaver and fish. Elsewhere there is evidence for sheep, always a success on cleared downland, and goats. The area's soil has now been cultivated for over 5,000 years and has lost most of its humus and loess content. In Neolithic times it would have been much more fertile, producing such nutritious crops as pulses and beans. Actual plant remains and textile fragments from the Bronze Age have been found preserved in a unique location in the Stonehenge area: the damp conditions at the bottom of a 30m deep well known as the Wilsford shaft.

Using new techniques we now know the broad effects on the environment of the prehistoric activities. Most of the earliest Wessex farming was pastoral, with cultivation restricted to small plots. In early Neolithic times the forest clearings around Stonehenge expanded rapidly to exploit the rich soil. But by the later Neolithic period the dwindling woodland resources needed careful management. By the early Bronze Age sheep grazed large areas of established pasture. In fact the tree cover became so sparse that the landscape of 2,000 BC was beginning to assume the open appearance of today.

LEFT:
  CARVING, PERHAPS A SYMBOL FOR A 'MOTHER–GODDESS',
  ON THE INSIDE OF THE FOURTH TRILITHON.

RIGHT:
  THE VIEW ALONG THE ASTRONOMICAL AXIS OF STONEHENGE,
  TOWARDS THE POINT OF MIDSUMMER SUNRISE.

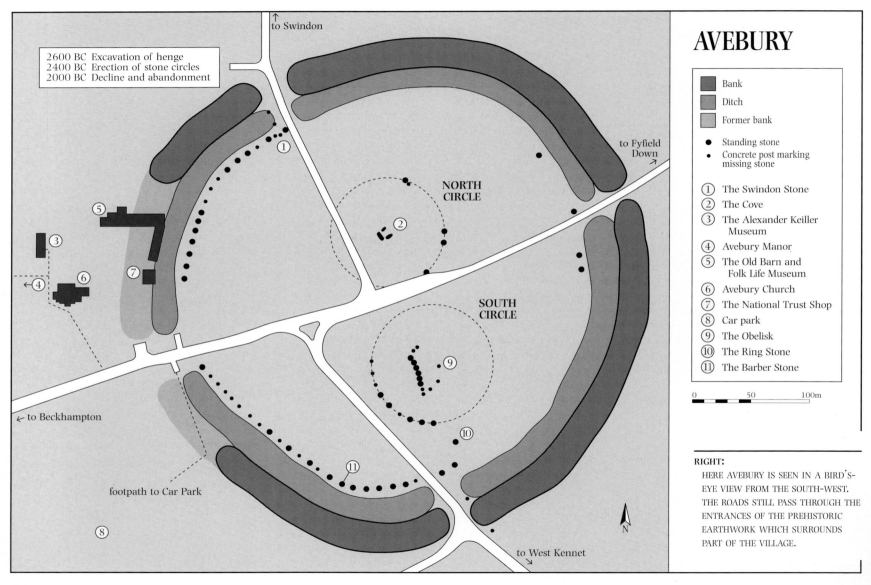

AVEBURY

2600 BC Excavation of henge
2400 BC Erection of stone circles
2000 BC Decline and abandonment

to Swindon

to Fyfield Down

NORTH CIRCLE

SOUTH CIRCLE

to Beckhampton

footpath to Car Park

to West Kennet

N

Bank

Ditch

Former bank

● Standing stone

• Concrete post marking missing stone

① The Swindon Stone
② The Cove
③ The Alexander Keiller Museum
④ Avebury Manor
⑤ The Old Barn and Folk Life Museum
⑥ Avebury Church
⑦ The National Trust Shop
⑧ Car park
⑨ The Obelisk
⑩ The Ring Stone
⑪ The Barber Stone

0   50   100m

AVEBURY

*I*n the 17th century, the antiquarian, John Aubrey, noted that Avebury far surpassed Stonehenge 'as a Cathedral doth a Parish Church'. Sir Richard Colt Hoare was also much impressed and wrote, in *Ancient Wiltshire* (1812): 'With awe and diffidence I enter the sacred precincts of this once hallowed sanctuary, the supposed parent of Stonehenge, the wonder of Britain and the most ancient, as well as the most interesting relict which our island can produce'. Of the four Wessex 'super-henges' (p.4) which are more than 300m across, Avebury's earthworks are by far the most impressive today. They also contain some of the largest megaliths in Britain and the great stone circle is the largest of its kind in Europe. The area has been inhabited by villagers for about 1,000 years. And so it comes as a surprise to learn that it remained unknown to outsiders until Aubrey rode through the village on a hunting trip in 1648.

Construction of the great henge

In about 2600 BC, or about 2,000 years after the first farmers reached Wessex, the building of Avebury began. They chose a lowland plain at the foot of the Marlborough Downs. Like most henges, the site is close to water, in this case the infant River Kennet. Using antlers as picks, the shoulder-bones of cattle as shovels, and woven baskets, gangs dug out the ditch and threw up the bank outside. The precise shape was not important. It would have been simple to define an exact circle with a rope stretched tight from the centre,

LEFT:
THE NEAREST STONE, CALLED THE BARBER STONE, NOW SET UPRIGHT, KILLED AN ITINERANT BARBER-SURGEON WHO WAS HELPING TO OVERTHROW IT EARLY IN THE FOURTEENTH CENTURY AD.

RIGHT:
THE NORTH-WEST QUARTER OF AVEBURY, WITH THE 65-TONNE SWINDON STONE IN THE FOREGROUND.

but it seems that the priests who first marked out the sacred enclosure were quite content to pace out a shapeless ring (see plan and photo on pp.21–22). If geometry was insignificant at this stage, the tremendous scale of the excavation was clearly vital. 120,000 cubic metres of solid chalk were dug from the ditch at Avebury, a volume about 60 times greater than the spoil from the ditch at Stonehenge. Only one earthwork can compare in size to Avebury, the 250,000 cubic metres of chalk and soil excavated to form Silbury Hill, just 1.5km to the south of Avebury. The two biggest Neolithic earthworks in Europe somehow form part of the same ritual landscape.

After digging at Windmill Hill, Alexander Keiller

bought Avebury and carried out a campaign of exemplary excavations through the 1930s. His team revealed how far the ditch has filled up since it was dug. When looking into the ditch today, visitors need to realize that it was first dug out no less than 6m below the present turf. Imagine the bank perhaps 5m higher than today, faced on the inside with a wall and gleaming white with fresh chalk, and you have some idea of its original appearance. The four modern roads still enter the henge through original gaps in the bank and causeways across the ditch. The West Kennet Avenue still leads into the south entrance and the former Beckampton Avenue began at the west entrance.

The stone circles

It has been estimated that there was originally a minimum of 247 standing stones within the henge and perhaps 400 more forming the two avenues outside. The heaviest remaining megalith, the Swindon Stone near the north entrance, weighs about 65 tonnes, but the survivors average about 15 tonnes. The Avebury stones are sarsens of the same geological type as those of Stonehenge. At Avebury, the sarsens were selected for their shape and used in their natural state, whereas at Stonehenge they were laboriously worked to a precise geometry. The Avebury builders preferred their stones to be either columnar or flat with a square or triangular outline.

The transport and erection of these stones in about 2400 BC represent one of the great triumphs of prehistoric building. Experts agree that they once lay on the surface of the surrounding hills and valleys, especially the Marlborough Downs. Neolithic and more modern builders have since removed all the natural boulders from the immediate surroundings but, if you follow Green Street out of the henge to the east, a chalk track will take you 3km to the main source area. There, on Fyfield Down, around map reference SU134706, natural sarsens still litter the lonely sheepwalks, although the heaviest ones were taken 4,000 years ago.

It is natural to wonder how the huge stones were moved and erected. A knowledge of the available tech-

nology makes wooden rollers the most likely method of transport, with the exact route carefully chosen to avoid steep and dangerous gradients. Once at their site, a small socket, only about 1m deep, was dug into the chalk and lined with wooden stakes which would help to guide the foot of the stone into the correct position. Ropes, wooden props and levers gradually raised the stone to the vertical in its socket. This was a laborious process – an experiment by Alexander Keiller's team in 1934 showed that 14 untrained men would take four days to erect one small flat stone using Neolithic methods. Great care was taken to place the centre of gravity directly over the middle of the hole. The final act was to ram a hard packing of chalk, flints and small sarsens around the base of the megalith to hold it firmly in its socket. The stability achieved is particularly impressive in the case of the giant Swindon Stone which has spent 4,000 years balanced on one corner with only a fragment of its bulk underground (p.28).

The builders chose to raise three sacred circles inside their temple. Despite their popular name, prehistoric stone circles are rarely circular. This is certainly true of the Great Circle, which follows the irregular plan of the henge, keeping a constant distance from the inner lip of the ditch. Originally it must have consisted of about 98 stones, but their partial destruction means that we can no longer tell whether the columnar and triangular shapes were placed at random or in some meaningful pattern. The huge size of the Great Circle allows ample space within it for the two separate circles, while in turn each of these could accommodate Stonehenge. In contrast with the general outline of Avebury, they are both exactly circular. The sequence of erection of the three circles remains unclear.

Both of the inner circles have the same diameter (103.6m). According to Alexander Thom's theory of prehistoric surveying, this is exactly 125 'megalithic yards' and the builders used in these circles a value for π of 3.140, only 1 part in 1,975 from the true value. Although they are the same size, the two circles contain very different ritual features. The centre of the southern circle was emphasized by an obelisk, a particularly tall stone with a height of 6.4m. Its site is now marked by a plinth. Stukeley drew it lying on the ground in 1723, but all that was left for Keiller to record in the 1930s was the large burning pit used to break it up. A similar fate befell 24 of the 29 stones that were once equally spaced around the southern circle. It is rare for any feature to mark the centre of a stone circle. The obelisk is made more unusual by forming the centre of a mysterious D-shaped setting of small rough sarsens, the so-called 'Z' feature, which partly survives.

The northern circle is just as fragmentary – only four stones survive from the original 27 – but the ritual element at its centre is more complete. The rectangular cove survives as a three-sided setting of stones. The 'Devil's Brandirons', to use its popular name, probably imitated the burial stall of a megalithic chambered tomb. But instead of being hidden under the dark earth of a barrow, the Avebury cove is a giant niche open to the sky, the setting for some public ritual of death. Such rites seem to have been widespread: other coves, such as Stanton Drew in Somerset or Stenness in the Orkney Isles, either lie within or close to stone circles.

The Avebury temple remained in active use for about 700 years. Towards the end of this period, c.2000 BC, the 75 Stonehenge sarsens were collected

LEFT:
THE SOUTH-WEST QUARTER OF THE HENGE, SEEN FROM THE SOUTH ENTRANCE.
RIGHT:
THE VIEW FROM THE SOUTH CIRCLE TO THE SOUTH ENTRANCE TOWARDS THE DISTANT SANCTUARY.

26

from the rich source on the Marlborough Downs. The
difficulty of fording the River Kennet further down-
stream raises the fascinating possibility that these
sarsens were a gift from the Avebury people and
passed through their completed temple for the priests
to sanctify them. Rodney Castleden believes it likely
that the Beckhampton Avenue was actually built to
celebrate the first mile of their long and ponderous
journey to Stonehenge.

The Avebury rituals

While Stonehenge was dedicated to the worship of
the moon and the sun, the meaning of the Avebury
temple seems instead strongly connected with the
great human themes of fertility, life and death. Rich
evidence of funerary feasts has been found at the

Sanctuary, which was linked by a procession route, the West Kennet Avenue, to the henge. The columnar and triangular stones of this avenue were deliberately paired together. Such a strong sexual symbolism implies a close connection between fertility and funerary rites. This celebration of the cycle of birth, life and death was a central part of Neolithic philosophy which is consistent with the symbolism found in megalithic passage graves of the same period. We could conclude that the rites at Avebury were intended to bring life to the dead and good fortune to the living.

Avebury's ritual landscape

The ceremonial landscape around Avebury is perhaps even richer than the Stonehenge environs. The main elements are: the West Kennet long barrow, with its magnificent stone chambered interior (in use from 3700 to 2200 BC); the unchambered Beckhampton Road long barrow (3250 BC); the large causewayed camp on Windmill Hill (3300 BC); the Sanctuary, a temple on Overton Hill (three phases, from 3000 to 2500 BC); the gigantic Silbury Hill mound (three phases, from 2700 to 2500 BC); the double avenues of standing stones to the Sanctuary and Beckhampton (2400 BC); and finally the numerous round barrows on the surrounding ridges (c.1800 BC).

Over the last 1,000 years, zealous Christians or greedy and ignorant farmers have destroyed or buried many of the standing stones in this landscape; the two circles at the Sanctuary, both of the avenues and the three circles of the great henge have all suffered. Some stones were broken up with fire and water; others were toppled and buried. Stukeley witnessed some of this damage in the 1720s. One culprit, a medieval barber-surgeon, died in the act of destruction, crushed under a falling megalith at Avebury in about 1325 – we can date his death from the coins found in his purse. Some of these stones, especially those in the West Kennet

THE MYSTERIOUS SILBURY HILL SEEN FROM NEAR THE WEST
KENNET LONG BARROW. ITS ENORMOUS SIZE (325,000 CU M)
IS A CENTRAL FEATURE OF AVEBURY'S LANDSCAPE.

Avenue, were re-erected in the 1930s. Since then, probing has shown that other stones still remain underground. The reconstruction on page 29, of a ritual during Avebury's heyday, shows how the monument appeared with all its stones in place. Today the circle survives best in the north-west quadrant (p.23).

No guidebook including Avebury could end without airing speculation about the ritual significance of the even larger earthwork so close at hand. Silbury Hill excites our wonder as a Neolithic engineering triumph: its complex network of internal retaining walls still prevents the rubble-fill from slumping. It superficially resembles a gigantic Bronze Age barrow, but we now know it was built 1,000 years earlier and contains no burials. Was it a harvest hill, symbolizing the earth-goddess pregnant with each year's new crops? Other Neolithic harvest hills built to ensure good fortune for the living may exist in the grounds of nearby Marlborough College, 10km down the River Kennet, or far away at Clifford Hill near Northampton.

Many will disagree with these interpretations. Archaeology is not an exact science and the evidence is sparse for ceremonies in Avebury's sacred enclosure because the priests kept the site clean during the centuries of its use. Some have seen the communities at the two great temples as rivals, but the apparent gift of the sarsens to Stonehenge would seem to show how closely they collaborated. Many intriguing mysteries await the reader who looks deeper than a short guidebook can into the questions raised by the ritual landscapes that surround the two temples. For instance, the medieval monk Geoffrey of Monmouth, an incorrigible inventor of history, told a story of how the magician Merlin moved Stonehenge from a mountain in Ireland by sea and river. Did Geoffrey somehow know the true story of how the bluestones came from a mountain on the way to Ireland?

31

FURTHER READING

Atkinson, Richard. *Stonehenge* (Harmondsworth, Penguin, 1979)

Burl, Aubrey. *Prehistoric Avebury* (New Haven, Yale U.P., 1979)

Rites of the Gods (London, Dent, 1981)

Prehistoric Astronomy and Ritual (Aylesbury, Shire, 1983)

The Stonehenge People (London, Dent, 1987)

Prehistoric Henges (Princes Risborough, Shire, 1991)

Castleden, Rodney. *The Stonehenge People* (London, Routledge & Kegan Paul, 1987)

Malone, Caroline. *Avebury* (London, B.T. Batsford Ltd/English Heritage, 1989)

Richards, Julian. *Stonehenge* (London, B.T. Batsford Ltd/English Heritage, 1991)

Thom, Alexander. *Megalithic Sites in Britain* (Oxford, Clarendon Press, 1967)

LEFT:

THE LONGSTONES, OR ADAM AND EVE, NEAR BECKHAMPTON. THE NEARER STONE WAS PERHAPS PART OF STUKELEY'S BECK-HAMPTON AVENUE, AND THE FURTHER PART OF A CIRCLE OR 'COVE'.

BACK COVER:

THE EAST SIDE OF STONEHENGE, SHOWING THE GREATER HEIGHT OF THE TRILITHONS (LEFT) AND THE CURVATURE OF THEIR LINTELS.

ACKNOWLEDGEMENTS

The photographs in this book are © Pitkin Pictorials by John Green, except p.3 Chorley & Handford, p.21 Aerofilms, pp.2, 6, 7 Salisbury Museum and p.31 Mick Sharp Photography.

Designed by John Buckley.

Illustrations on pp.5 & 29 © Jonothan Potter 1994.
Line drawings on inside front cover and p.20 based on original illustrations by H. Mason.

Text © Pitkin Pictorials 1994.

Publication in this form © Pitkin Pictorials 1994, reprinted 1995.

The author acknowledges the work of Professor Richard Atkinson, Dorothy Bosomworth, Dr Aubrey Burl and Dr David Price-Williams in the preparation of the text for this book.

Printed in Great Britain

ISBN 0 85372 710 4   295/20